My Little Book
Cars

by Rod Green

QED

Quarto is the authority on a wide range of topics.
Quarto educates, entertains and enriches the lives of
our readers—enthusiasts and lovers of hands-on living.
www.quartoknows.com

Publisher: Maxime Boucknooghe
Editorial Director: Victoria Garrard
Art Director: Miranda Snow
Project Editor: Joanna McInerney
Design and editorial: Tall Tree Ltd

Words in **bold** are explained in the glossary on page 60.

First published in the UK in 2016 by
QED Publishing
A Quarto Group company
The Old Brewery
6 Blundell Street
London N7 9BH

www.quartoknows.com/brand/979/QED-Publishing/

A catalogue record for this book is available from the British Library

ISBN 978 1 78493 463 7

Printed in China

Contents

Car parts

Cars have been around for 130 years. Modern cars still work in much the same way as **vintage** cars.

>> Beneath the body we can see the engine, gearbox, drive shaft and rear axle.

<< Early cars looked like carriages **with engines instead of horses.**

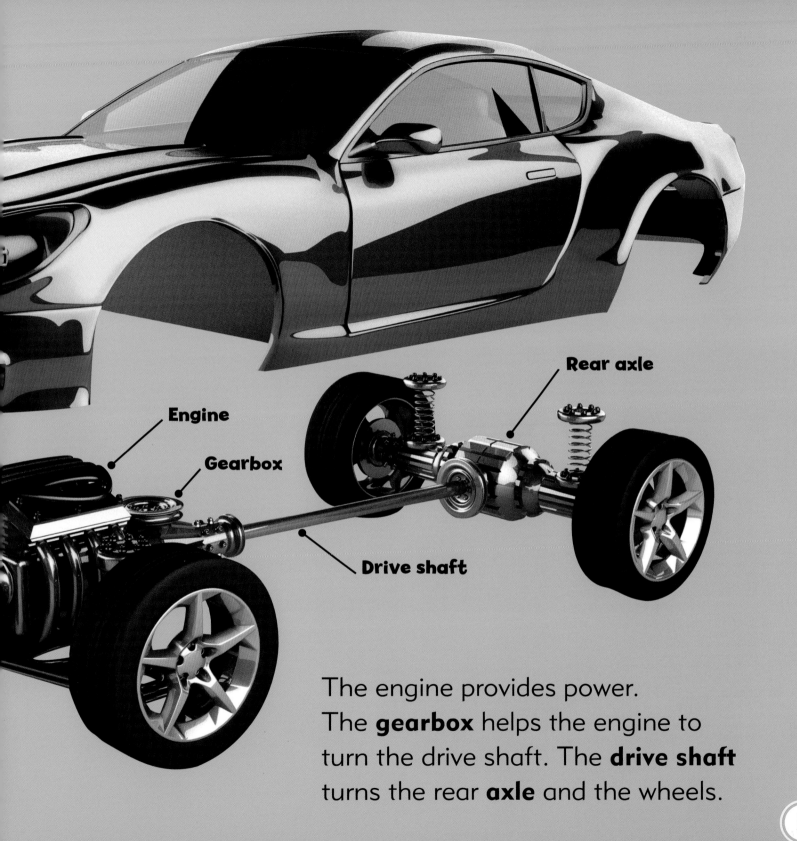

Rear axle

Engine

Gearbox

Drive shaft

The engine provides power.
The **gearbox** helps the engine to
turn the drive shaft. The **drive shaft**
turns the rear **axle** and the wheels.

Front engine

In most cars, the engine sits at the front. The engine powers the front wheels, the back wheels or all four wheels.

<< **The engine bay of this Ford Mustang is packed with** components.

Engines are made of thousands of separate parts. A car engine can weigh up to 250 kilogrammes – more than two adult passengers.

>> In this Dodge Challenger, the engine powers just the rear wheels.

^ This Volkswagen Golf's engine powers just the front wheels.

Rear engine

Some cars have the engine in the rear, behind the passengers and the rear axle.

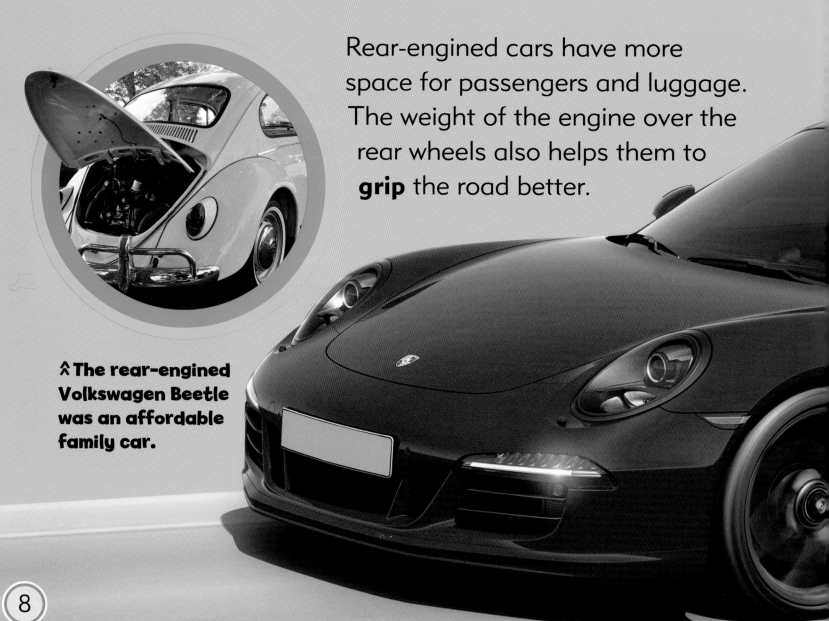

Rear-engined cars have more space for passengers and luggage. The weight of the engine over the rear wheels also helps them to **grip** the road better.

⌃ **The rear-engined Volkswagen Beetle was an affordable family car.**

>> This cutaway of a Porsche 911 shows its engine behind the rear axle.

⌄ **The Porsche 911 is a** high-performance **rear-engined car.**

Mid engine

Mid-engined cars have their engines between the front and the rear wheels.

Many high-performance sports cars, such as the Pagani Huayra, have a mid-engined layout. It gives the car excellent balance.

>> Good balance and grip help the Huayra to drive through bends at higher speeds without skidding.

>> **Beneath the Huayra's** bodywork its engine sits in front of the rear axle.

Steam cars

The first road vehicles that were not pulled by horses were powered by steam engines.

« **This French steam** quadricycle, **built in 1887, was one of the first steam cars.**

>> This American Stanley steam car dates from 1912. It reached speeds of more than 100 kilometres per hour.

The engine of a steam car was powered by steam made by heating up water. It took some time to heat the water, so the cars did not start straight away.

<< In 2009 the British steam car, Inspiration, set a world record speed for steam cars of 239 kilometres per hour.

Electric cars

Electric cars are powered by electric **motors**. The cars carry batteries to run the motors.

↑ **New York City had electric cabs in 1897.**

The first electric cars were made in the 19th century. They were slow and could only travel short distances.

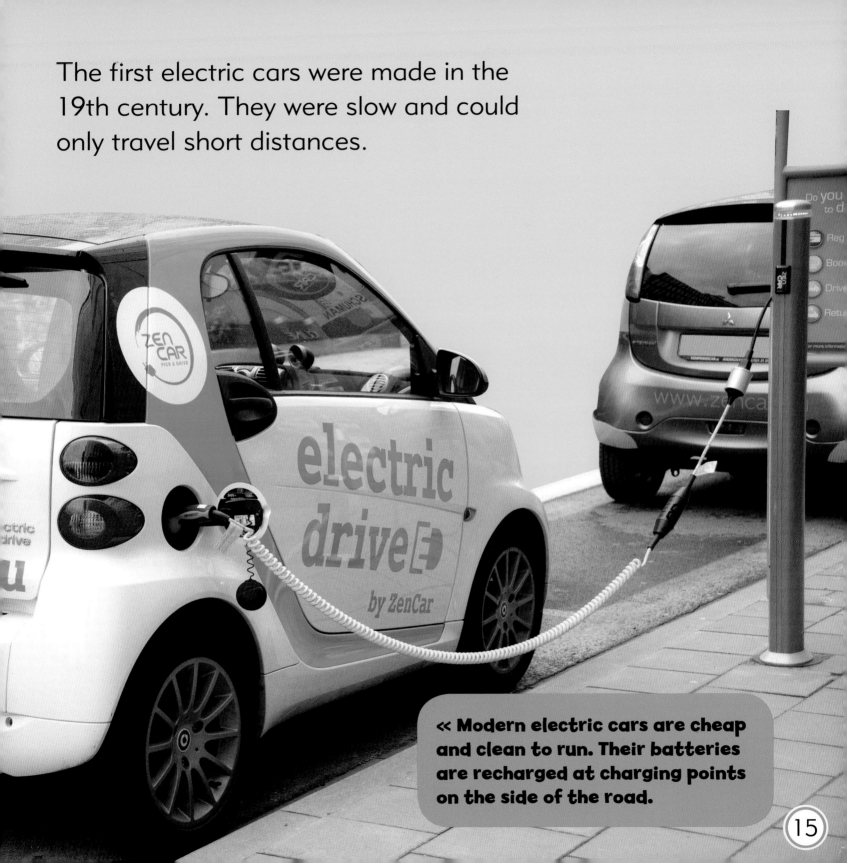

« Modern electric cars are cheap and clean to run. Their batteries are recharged at charging points on the side of the road.

Petrol power

The first petrol engines were noisy and unreliable. They were soon improved and became the most popular engines for cars.

⌄ Early cars had to be started by turning a handle at the front.

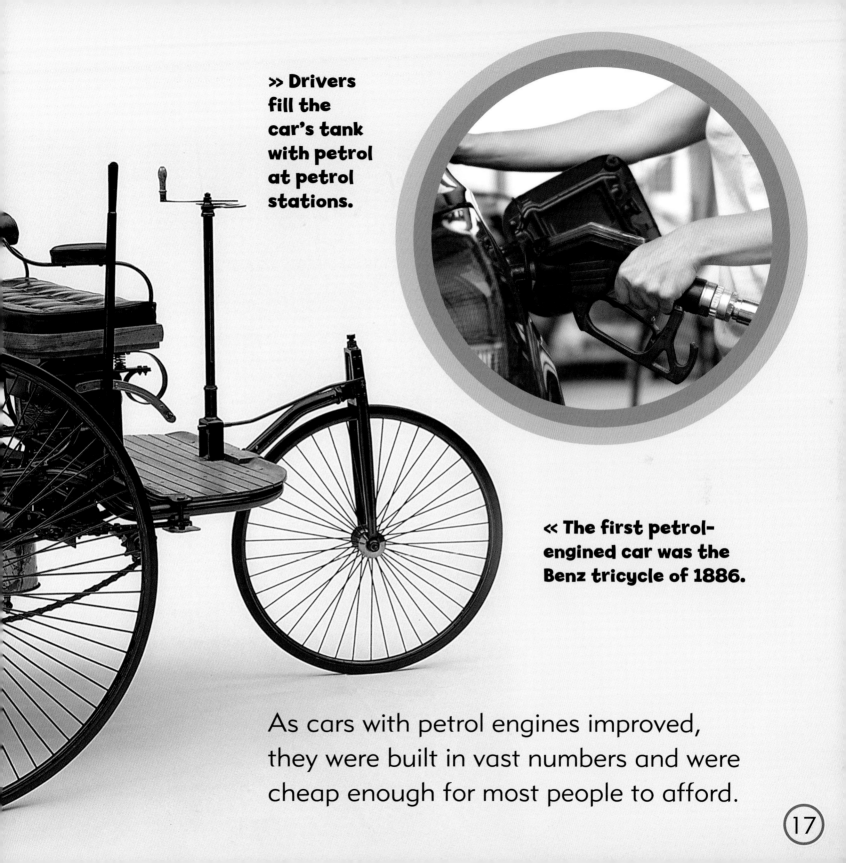

>> Drivers fill the car's tank with petrol at petrol stations.

<< The first petrol-engined car was the Benz tricycle of 1886.

As cars with petrol engines improved, they were built in vast numbers and were cheap enough for most people to afford.

Hybrid cars

A hybrid car is powered by both a petrol engine and an electric motor.

⌃ **The Lohner Porsche of 1900 had electric motors in each wheel.**

Electric motor

Hybrid cars use their electric motors while in town. This keeps them quiet and clean. The petrol engine provides extra power when driving faster or over long distances.

⌄ The Porsche 918 Spyder has two electric motors and a powerful petrol engine.

⌃ The Toyota Prius is the world's most popular hybrid car.

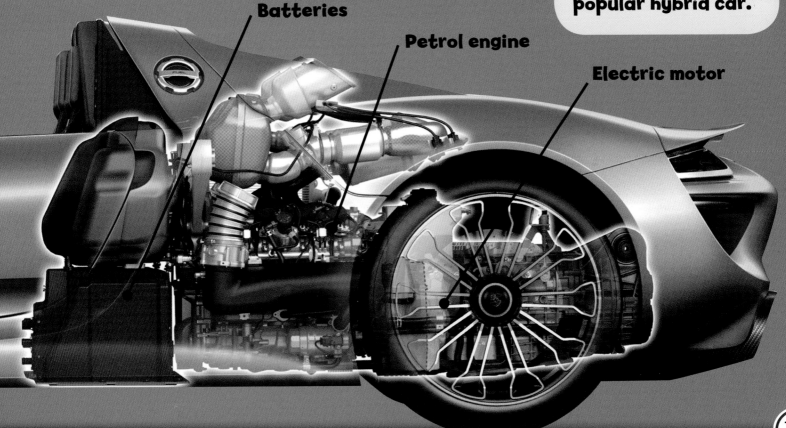

Batteries

Petrol engine

Electric motor

City cars

Designed to be driven in heavy traffic, these cars are small and easy to park.

City cars are small, but most have room inside for four adults as well as a **boot** for luggage. They have small engines, so they don't use much fuel.

>> City cars are ideal for parking in tight spaces.

« City cars called hatchbacks have a big rear door to make it easy to load the boot.

» The rear-engined Fiat 500 was first produced in 1957.

Family cars

Family cars are big enough to carry up to five people in comfort.

Designed to take an average family on local trips or longer holiday journeys, family cars have lots of space for luggage.

⌄ **This Ford Focus is described as an** estate. **It has a long boot to carry bulky luggage.**

« Most modern cars have sat-nav. A screen shows the driver which route to take.

⌃ Large objects such as bicycles can be carried on the roof of a family car.

People carriers

People carriers are really big cars that are ideal for large families.

⌄ **People carriers such as this Nissan Serena have enough room inside for up to eight people and their luggage.**

« **Side doors slide open wide for easy access.**

People carriers are not only for family transport. They are also used as taxis, or **limousines**, with space for passengers to hold business meetings while they are on the road.

⌃ The seats line up in rows, but the passenger seats can be arranged to face each other.

SUVs

Sports Utility Vehicles, or SUVs, are cars for people who enjoy outdoor activities.

An SUV needs to be tough, as its driver may want to take it across open countryside. SUVs have all-wheel drive, which means that the engine powers all four wheels.

« SUVs are ideal for snowy or icy conditions, where their extra power keeps them out of trouble.

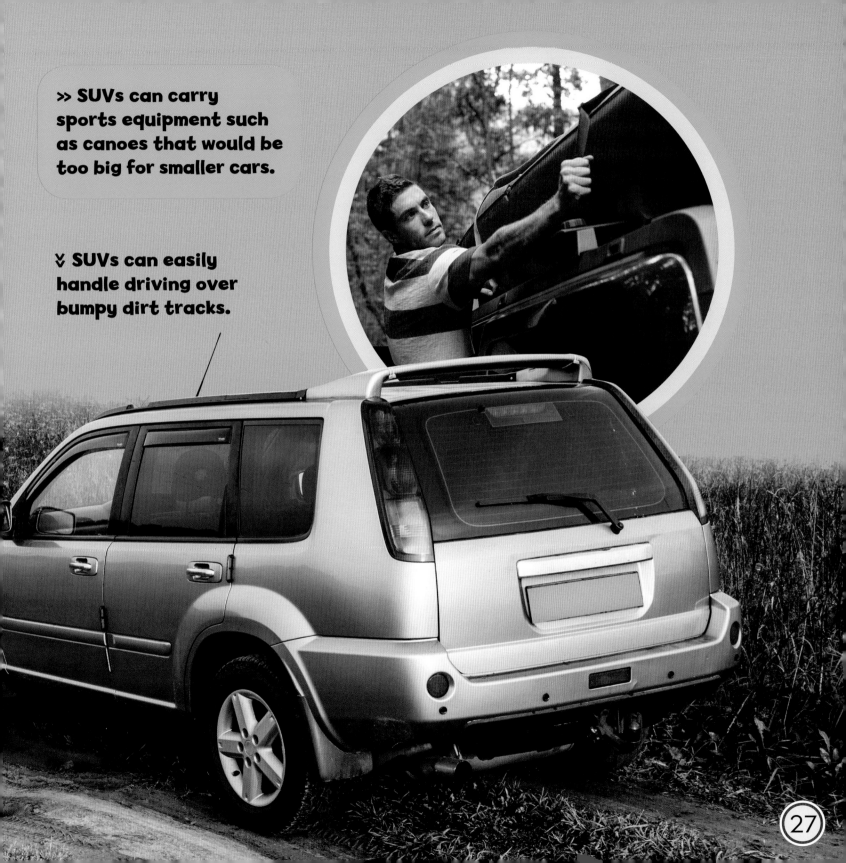

>> SUVs can carry sports equipment such as canoes that would be too big for smaller cars.

⌄ SUVs can easily handle driving over bumpy dirt tracks.

Off-road vehicles

Off-road vehicles have to be able to go where no other car can.

⌄ The original Jeep was used in the Second World War. It carried soldiers and equipment around war zones.

« This Jeep has big wheels and chunky tyres for extra grip on slippery slopes.

Off-road vehicles need all-wheel drive and powerful engines to help them climb steep slopes, cross rivers or plough through deep mud or snow.

« Lightweight racers called sandrails can hurtle up and down desert sand dunes.

Luxury cars

Designed for travelling in total comfort, luxury cars are large and expensive.

Everything about a luxury car has to be the absolute best, which makes them cost more than other cars. A Rolls-Royce Wraith costs as much as at least ten average cars.

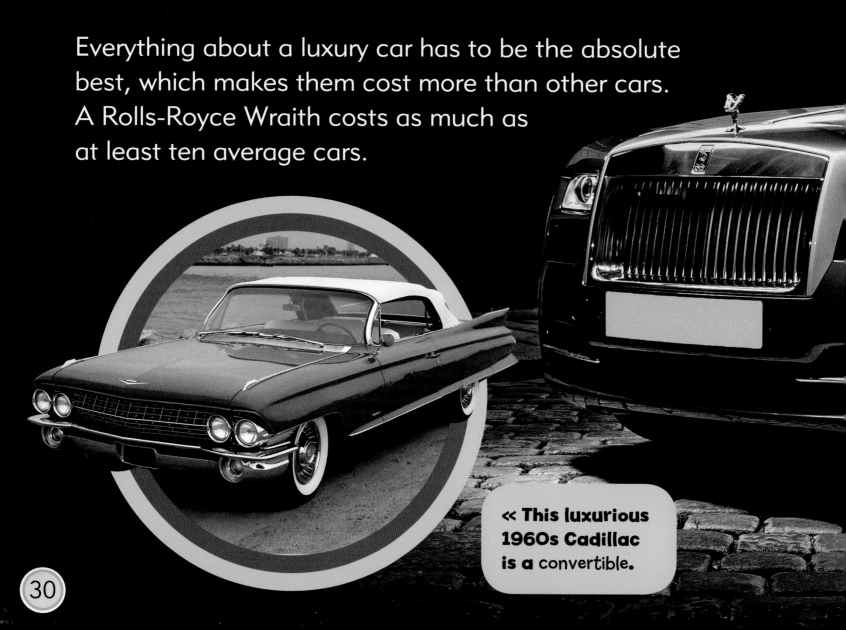

« This luxurious 1960s Cadillac is a convertible.

>> The Wraith's seats are made from the very finest quality leather and the roof is lit like a starry sky.

<< The Wraith is quiet but also very fast. It has a top speed of 250 kilometres per hour.

Emergency vehicles

Emergency services such as **paramedics** need fast cars with lots of space for equipment.

LIFEGUARD

« The rear of this paramedic's estate car is packed with medical equipment.

Estate cars and SUVs make ideal emergency vehicles. They start out as normal cars but are then fitted with sirens, flashing lights and life-saving equipment.

⌃ This GMC Sierra is adapted for the fire brigade. It has space for fire-fighting equipment.

« Lifeguards use this all-wheel-drive Ford Escape to speed safely across sandy beaches.

Police cars

Police forces all over the world use cars in a number of different ways.

The first police car was a basic electric vehicle used in Akron, Ohio, USA, in 1899. It had a top speed of 26 kilometres per hour. Today's police cars are much faster and use the latest technology.

« This Lamborghini is used to catch speeding supercars on Italian motorways.

>> Police speeding to emergencies in snowy or icy conditions need cars like this all-wheel-drive Range Rover.

>> In crowded cities, police may use cars as small as this two-seat, electric Renault Twizy.

Limousines

Limousines are large luxury cars used on special occasions or to transport very important passengers.

A limousine is usually driven by a **chauffeur**. The driver's compartment is separated from the passengers by a glass screen.

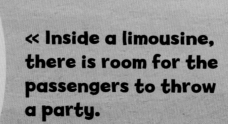

« Inside a limousine, there is room for the passengers to throw a party.

>> The President of the United States travels in a limousine that is bullet and bomb proof.

ʌ Stretch limousines have enough space to carry up to 20 passengers.

Movie stars

Cars and movies were developed around the same time, at the beginning of the 20th century.

<< **Bumblebee from the *Transformers* movie could change into a Chevrolet Camaro.**

>> **A new Batmobile was created for the *Batman vs Superman* movie.**

Car chases and stunts have been used in movies since the early 1900s. From *Chitty Chitty Bang Bang* to the latest James Bond film, a car now features in the action in many movies.

ʌ **The Weasley brothers rescued Harry Potter in a small, flying Ford Anglia.**

Formula 1 racing cars

These fast, powerful racing cars use the very latest technology.

The single-seat cars are mid-engined and run on smooth, slick tyres when it is dry. On wet, slippery tracks tyres with deep grooves are used, which give extra grip.

« **The cars race on purpose-built race tracks.**

>> During a race, a car can have fresh tyres fitted in under 10 seconds.

<< Modern Formula 1 cars have electric motors as well as petrol engines to give them extra power.

Endurance racing cars

In endurance racing, competitors drive as far as they can in a set time period, usually six, 12 or even 24 hours.

Different types of car race at the same time, on the same track. The types are divided into 'classes' and you can be first in your class without coming first overall in the race.

« Races carry on through the night and even cars without roofs race in the rain.

« When a car stops for fuel, a new driver takes over as they can drive for only four hours at a time.

« Cars like this Ginetta-Nissan are the fastest, with top speeds of more than 320 kilometres per hour.

Saloon car racing

These racing cars look like ordinary cars but have more powerful engines.

To save weight, the cars have no carpets or other fittings but they do have **roll cages** to protect the driver if the car should flip over in a crash.

« **Drivers wear helmets and special racing harness seatbelts.**

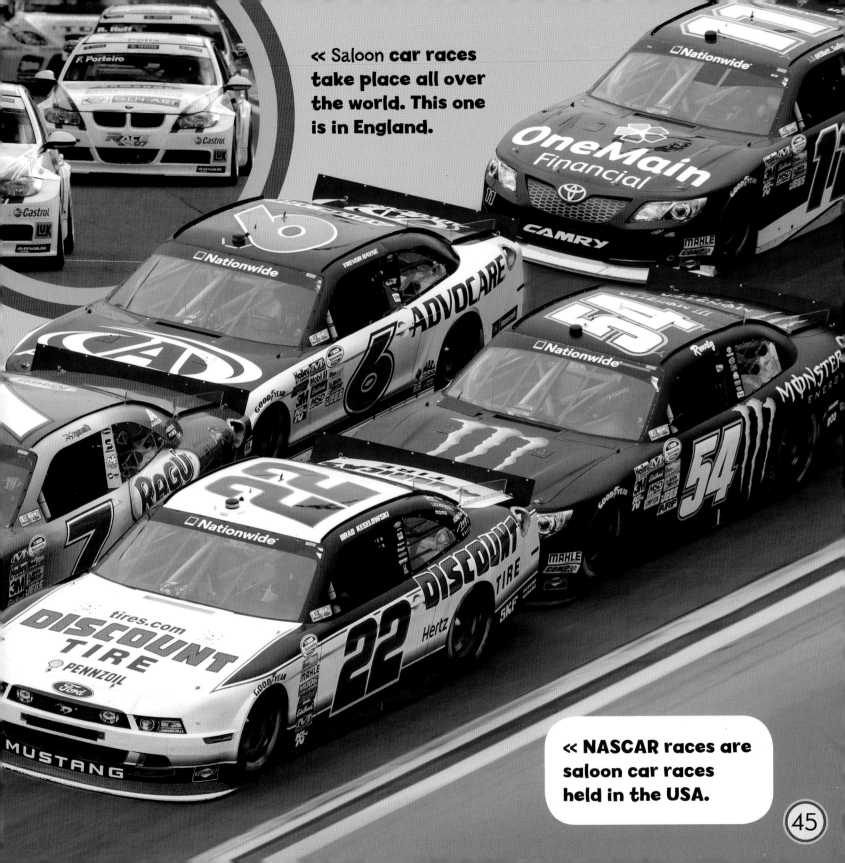

<< Saloon **car races** take place all over the world. This one is in England.

<< NASCAR races are saloon car races held in the USA.

45

Rally cars

Rally cars compete over special courses to see who can finish in the fastest time.

A rally car has a co-driver who studies the route before the race and tells the driver what sort of bends or hazards are coming up.

« The cars must cope with extreme heat in desert races.

>> Cars are reinforced so that they can take humps and bumps at high speeds.

<< In winter or on mountain tracks, the cars race on snow and ice.

Drag racing

Drag races are straight-line sprints where the drivers aim to set a fast time on a short stretch of track.

^ **The cars race along the track in pairs.**

The fastest drag racers are called Top Fuel. The Top Fuel cars can cover a 300-metre track in less than 4 seconds.

« Top Fuel dragsters can reach speeds of 500 kilometres per hour.

∧ At the end of their sprint, the cars use parachutes to slow them down.

Vintage cars

Vintage cars are cars that were made many years ago. If properly looked after, they can still be driven.

<< In 2007, a 1937 Mercedes-Benz 540 roadster sold for £5.3 million.

Old cars can be extremely valuable because they are very rare, like antiques. The cars are sold at **auctions**, where collectors pay huge sums to own a piece of motoring history.

« A Rolls-Royce like this from 1904 was sold in 2007 for £4.7 million.

« The world's most expensive car is not old enough to be called vintage. A 1962 Ferrari 250 GTO sold in 2014 for over £25 million.

Longest cars

Long cars have always been the most elegant way to travel, giving passengers more space inside.

>> **This French Bugatti Royale from the 1930s has an overall length of 6.4 metres.**

>> The Mercedes Maybach Pullman is the world's longest production car at almost 6.5 metres.

Passengers enjoy a smoother ride in long cars. In shorter cars, the rear wheels hit a bump at almost the same time as the front wheels, which makes the car bounce more.

>> This 1934 Cadillac Fleetwood is 6.1 metres long.

Smallest cars

Some cars are so tiny that they make small city cars look as big as limousines!

« The three-wheeled Peel P50 is the world's smallest car. It has one seat and one door.

⌃ The rear-engined Smart Fortwo has two seats and two doors. It is the world's most popular small car.

Small cars don't need such powerful engines as larger cars. This means that they use less fuel, they are cheaper to run and they produce less pollution.

Fastest cars

The world's fastest road cars are the sleek, futuristic supercars. Some are quicker than Formula 1 racing cars.

>> **The top speed of the Koenigsegg Agera One:1 is 440 kilometres per hour.**

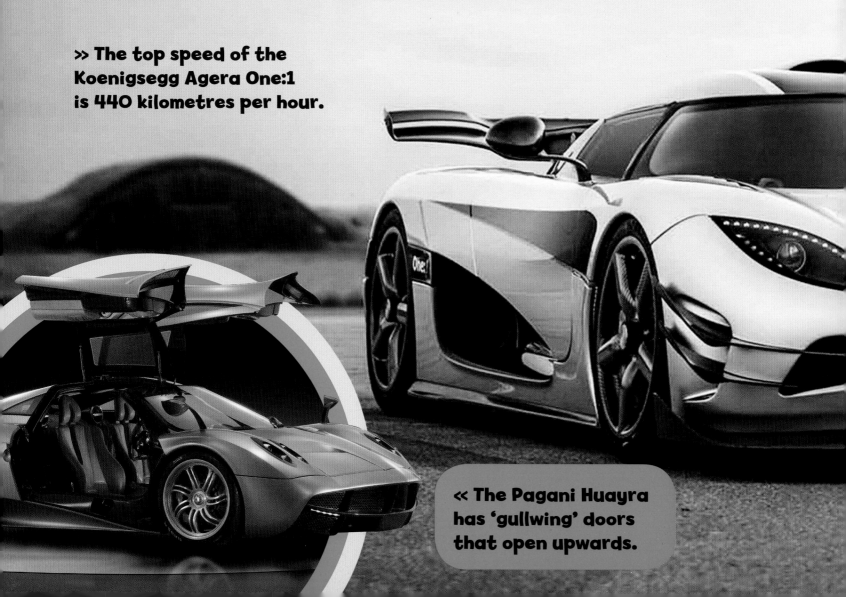

<< **The Pagani Huayra has 'gullwing' doors that open upwards.**

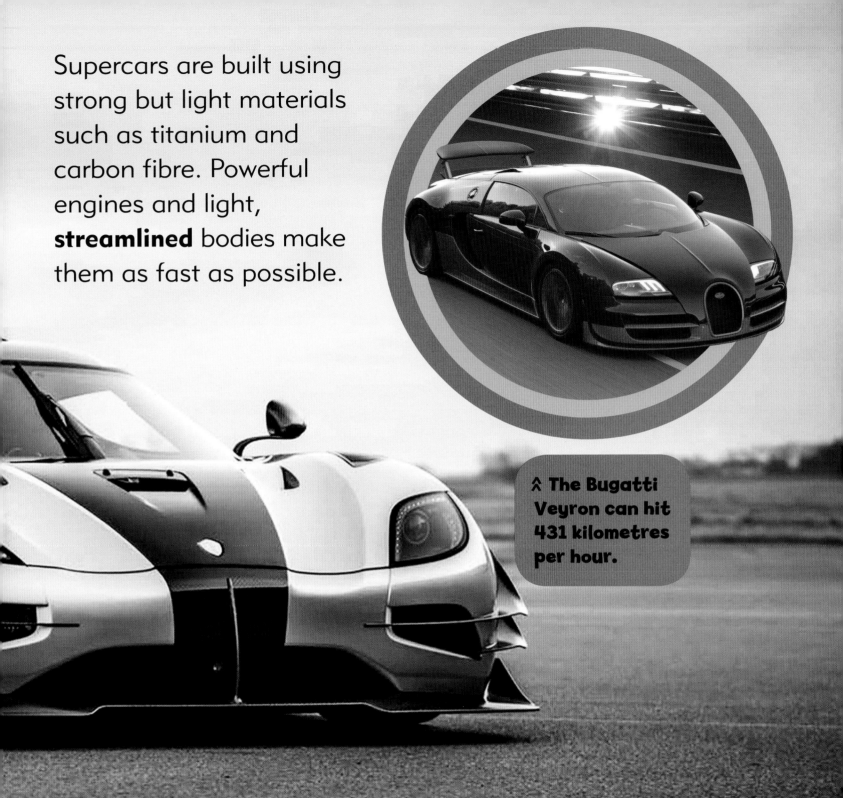

Supercars are built using strong but light materials such as titanium and carbon fibre. Powerful engines and light, **streamlined** bodies make them as fast as possible.

⌃ The Bugatti Veyron can hit 431 kilometres per hour.

The land speed record

For more than 100 years, car makers have competed for the title of fastest car ever.

« In 1899, the French car *La Jamais Contente* was the first car to travel at more than 100 kilometres per hour.

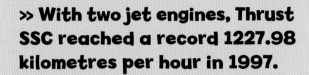
>> With two jet engines, Thrust SSC reached a record 1227.98 kilometres per hour in 1997.

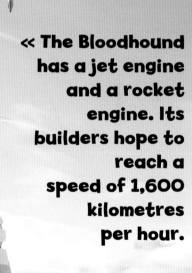

To set the World Land Speed Record, a car is timed to see how fast it completes a measured course. The car is already travelling at speed when it crosses the starting line.

<< The Bloodhound has a jet engine and a rocket engine. Its builders hope to reach a speed of 1,600 kilometres per hour.

Castrol EDGE

Rolls-Royce

RC serco

JAGUAR

Glossary

auction A sale at which buyers bid against each other.

axle A rod that connects the wheels of a car to one another.

bodywork The panels that create a car's shape.

boot A storage area at the back of a car.

carriage A horse-drawn vehicle with wheels.

chauffeur A professional driver.

components Individual parts of a machine or device.

convertible A car with a removable roof.

drive shaft Rods that connect the engine to the gearbox, and the gearbox to the wheels.

estate A car with a large boot reaching up to the roof, and a door at the rear.

gearbox A system of cogs that transfers power from the engine to the wheels.

grip The force of a car's wheels touching the road.

high-performance Able to reach high speeds quickly and to take corners easily.

limousine A luxury car that is used on special occasions.

motor A machine that creates movement.

parachute Cloth that fills with air to slow the movement of a person or a vehicle.

paramedics Workers who provide care in emergencies such as accidents.

quadricycle A light vehicle with four wheels.

roll cage A steel frame inside a racing car to protect the driver.

saloon A car with a boot that is separate from the occupants.

sat-nav Short for satellite navigation. Gives a driver directions by tracking the car's position using satellites.

streamlined Shaped to allow air to flow easily over the body.

vintage An old car made before the Second World War.

Index

Picture Credits

(t=top, b=bottom, l=left, r=right, c=centre)

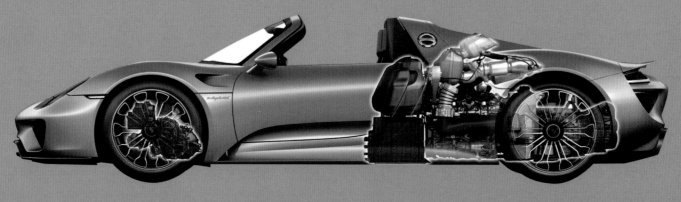